Reflections on VIET NAM

DIALOGUE PRESS, INC.
BERKELEY & NEW YORK
1991

ISBN 0-9630136-0-2
Copyright, 1989, 1991
DIALOGUE PRESS, INC.
Box 45
1678 Shattuck Avenue
Berkeley, CA 94709

PUBLISHER'S NOTE

The essays you hold in your hands were written by members of the Yale College Class of 1964 who were in Vietnam during the late 1960s and early 1970s and by the widow of one of their classmates, Bruce W. Warner. The essays are reprinted from *Later Life,* the 25th Reunion Classbook of the Yale Class of 1964, edited by Robert G. Kaiser and Jethro K. Lieberman and published in May, 1989.

In the aftermath of a different war in a different place at a different time, these essays are offered as a mournful and monitory reminder of the dreadful costs of a venture now seemingly so long ago. We forget at our peril.

September, 1991

CONTENTS

VERY UGLY, VERY MEAN, VERY STUPID
Robert G. Kaiser
7

SOUTH VIETNAM, 1966-1969
T. M. (Mac) Deford
11

MISCARRIAGE: REFLECTIONS ON A WAR
William M. Drennen, Jr.
23

A LETTER ON VIETNAM
John S. Wilbur, Jr.
39

BRUCE
Mimo Robinson
45

A NOTE ON CONTRIBUTORS
51

VERY UGLY, VERY MEAN, VERY STUPID

❧   Robert G. Kaiser

Surely one of the most talented Yale graduates of our time is Maya Ying Lin, the Yale architecture student whose design for the Vietnam Memorial on the mall in Washington won a national competition, and was built in the shadow of Abraham Lincoln's parthenon. What an amazing structure it is—so palpably a monument to defeat, so unremittingly brutal in the way it reminds every visitor of the cost of that war. The cost was not the billions spent, of course; it was those 50,000 young lives, the lives of our contemporaries, squandered to redeem first the errors, and then the vanities, of powerful men. Maya Lin's black granite scar on the mall, listing the name of every victim, is the memorial those powerful men deserve.

The names of only a handful of our classmates appear on that wall. The overriding majority of the class never had to serve. We were just a little too old to face the worst of it, and we were well equipped to dodge Vietnam by becoming parents or professors or scheming other alternatives to the draft. Mine was a bad back.

REFLECTIONS ON VIETNAM

But almost as soon as I got the 1-Y draft status I had so ardently sought, I began trying to get to Vietnam. Not as a soldier, to be sure—I knew I wanted to avoid that—but as a reporter. It struck me then, as it strikes me now, that Vietnam would be the critical event for our generation. I wanted to see it, to know it. My efforts bore fruit in early 1969, when The Washington Post agreed to send an almost 26-year-old to join the two-man Saigon bureau.

Letters and notes saved from my 18 months in the war reveal my excessive reliance on the word "crazy" to describe the scene that surrounded us there. But it was apt! Hannah was one of only a few American wives then present in Saigon. We lived in a rather grand apartment over a car dealership in the heart of the city. I could go to war by day, flying by helicopter to the scene of battle or just to see the situation in the countryside, and return in time for a martini and dinner cooked by our Vietnamese servant (she is now a resident of Arlington, Virginia). I could spend the evening with infantrymen on a remote firebase, or at Ellsworth Bunker's residence for an elegant dinner. We actually belonged to a country club in Saigon, the Cercle Sportif, that the French had left behind—a pool, tennis courts, nice spot for a quick, light lunch. A South Vietnamese tank was stationed on the grounds, which abutted the presidential palace. *Good Morning, Vietnam* gave you a strong whiff of all this. It really was crazy.

The American soldiers there understood the craziness.

Robert G. Kaiser

They taught us all to remember the exact date of our arrival "in country" (March 23, 1969), so we could join in conversations about when they would be going back to "the world"—the happy moment that came for each soldier exactly 12 months after arrival. If home was "the world," then this place they were experiencing was something else—something other-worldly. Most of them had just one objective: to get out of there.

I have been surprised by the revival of interest in Vietnam that began with *Platoon*. For so long, I thought, experience in Vietnam was something that many shared, but almost no one discussed. Now the war is ubiquitous. And at last, with the publication of Neil Sheehan's brilliant *A Bright Shining Lie*, it has the book it deserved. I urged some of our classmates with Vietnam experience to record them for this volume, a request that elicited the contributions printed here.

My sense is that the war was critical partly because of the upheaval it caused, but more importantly because of the turning point it marked, particularly for our generation. Vietnam ended the American Century far ahead of schedule. The war taught us that happy-ever-after and boundless progress were American myths, not laws of nature.

Looking through my Vietnam stuff recently I found a copy of a letter I wrote from Saigon to my brother David in June of 1969, just as he was graduating from Harvard. It appears that I was saving carbons of my letters then with a 26-year-old's eye to posterity, or to memoirs. I wrote then:

REFLECTIONS ON VIETNAM

"... *Your generation (and mine too) grew up at the height— or in the depths—of the American dream. We were the world's good guys; we would salvage the dignity of a man; we would elect JFK when we needed a knight to fight for the downtrodden; America the Beautiful would even, finally, make room for its oppressed minorities. You and I and Mark Rudd got conned by that line. We started to believe that men were decent to each other by nature; that progress was a natural state of affairs; that bad things tended naturally to get better, and so forth. Then came, as it had to, a very difficult period. We stumbled stupidly into a messy war. Our flirtation with equal rights for blacks ran into a terrible barrier—the fact that white people were afraid of black people. We lost our white knight and got a folksy guy with a high boob quotient who was neither reassuring or, in the end, helpful. Then our friends started getting killed — dead, not another can of beer — in that war, and our grandparents or somebody (in our family it was Aunt __) who used to seem decent turned out to be a racist, and a few other things went wrong, and the world looked very ugly, very mean, very stupid. . . ."*

That sounds more cynical than I like to feel I am today— but only slightly. Watching my magnificent country struggle and fail in Vietnam was the greatest lesson of these 25 years.

SOUTH VIETNAM, 1966-1969

🌿 T. M. (Mac) Deford

Vietnam: a fragmented mosaic in my mind 20 years later, as it was even then. The intense blue of cloudless skies, the sun-yellow of vast sandy beaches, the lime green of maturing rice fields.

But also, metallic gray and blood red.

The analogy of Vietnam as a fragmented mosaic is not inappropriate. It was a puzzle—no one had an overview of all the pieces, no one knew what it was supposed to look like when finished, no one even was sure how many pieces there were.

I was lucky. I spent three years in Vietnam, the last half of which was of my own choosing—and the pieces of the mosaic I saw were usually the bright blues or yellows or the hypnotic greens, not, of course that the other uglier colors didn't occasionally intrude. I was a civilian there. When I arrived in the spring of 1966, there were only 50,000 Americans in the war; three years later, when I left, there were ten times that number. It was the key years of U.S. involvement, the time when the war went from being another foreign policy en-

REFLECTIONS ON VIETNAM

deavor into which we had inadvertently backed to the event which dominated America for half a generation.

Very few people I knew in Vietnam in those years thought the war was winnable the way we were doing it. Graphically, the line of discontent within the U.S. was growing considerably faster than the U.S. military was winning, which meant that Vietnamization became inevitable. We all, in country, had endless debates about the strategy to follow, but they basically came down to variations drawn from the above awareness, or contradiction, the solution to which—except for the wild-eyed right-wingers' idea of bombing the dikes and physically wiping out North Vietnam—inevitably meant getting the U.S. military out. Considering that I was there for three years, it is odd to recall that the first realization I had that U.S. forces were not the answer came within a month of my arrival.

At that time, I was living in Southern II Corps with a U.S. military training detachment that was working with a Vietnamese regional force center. Some of the area I was assigned to cover was considered insecure, including a string of hamlets along Route 1 near a special forces camp. Occasionally, the special forces would come into the district capital, a village of about 3,000, mostly ethnic tribal Chinese. I could take advantage of their road-clearing operations to go spend a few days with them. On one such trip—nothing ever worked out quite as it was supposed to anyway—I was unable to get back. A few Viet Cong were reported to be crossing the no-man's

T. M. Deford

land (free fire zone) nearby and an air strike was called in from Phan Rang. The spotter plane had an extra seat and the pilot said he could drop me off where I wanted to go after the strike; I could earn my passage by "spotting" for him. Unfortunately, or perhaps fortunately, there was nothing to spot —I remember several wayward buffalo but no "hooches," no movement, just a few paths crisscrossing the somewhat arid landscape. It was clear the air strike was not necessary but we fired off our tracer rockets at lean-tos, at the water buffalo, at anything that could have been remotely constructed as indicating human presence, and the fighters made pass after pass over the empty land. The pilot explained that the fighters would be less likely to come next time, when perhaps they would actually be needed, if it was all a mistake. He filed a report afterwards listing the nonexistent targets which had been destroyed. At the time, it was an exhilarating sight— the jets, a speck at first to the north rolling in under the high monsoon thunderheads, the noise and color as our tracers flashed earthward, the majestic, almost eagle-like, flight of the jets as they swooped down in a great curving arc, the rockets exploding beneath us while the planes leveled out and disappeared momentarily, riding up for another pass. It would, presumably, have been terrifying to have been on the ground, and perhaps it made an impression on some black-pajamaed guerrillas who had safely reached the foothills, but I had only been in Vietnam about six weeks and the episode was not reassuring: the casual way in which a costly and useless air strike was reported as a success and the futility, in any case, of using F-14s to go after a band of five or six VC moving from one hideaway to another, and then, at least an hour after the sighting. There were plenty of Montagnard troops around and even some district forces, but why bother when you can call in the Air Force.

A few months later, the 1st Cav moved into the southern part of the province for several weeks of joint clearing operations with Vietnamese soldiers. I participated in some of the on-going provincial level briefings—very little was permanently accomplished by the 1st Cav—and later at a full-stage review for General Westmoreland, where it was revealed that considerably more was accomplished.

I was subsequently to spend most of the following two years based in Saigon, where the experience of what I had seen at the district level gave me, and most other colleagues from the field, a cynical view of body counts and villages colored pacified on the large briefing maps.

A cynic within a month? Why in the world did I stay three years?

It was, oddly, very much an intellectual experience. We would spend half the night, many nights, the whole time I was there, arguing about what we were doing and for what purpose, and how, given the fact that we were there, we could accomplish our objectives.

Clearly and obviously to those of us in Vietnam, we were not there to save the South Vietnamese from communism.

T. M. Deford

In *realpolitik* terms, we stayed in Vietnam because of the belief in one form or another in the domino theory.

Obviously then, one says, we were wrong. South Vietnam lost, but besides Cambodia and Laos, which no one ever portrayed as of significant strategic importance, there were no dominoes. Nothing happened in 1975 that would not have happened in 1963, except for the deaths in the meantime of so many tens of thousands of Americans and so many hundreds of thousands of Vietnamese. Except, the world was an entirely different place by 1975. The Sino-Soviet split, which no doubt was already in train by the early '60s, had been pushed to such an extent by the next decade that China and Russia were virtual enemies when the war ended. Thailand had become strong and self-confident, as indeed had Indonesia, Malaysia, and even the Philippines. In all these countries, there had been varying degrees of communist threats in the late '50s and early '60s. How would these threats have developed if South Vietnam had been taken over by Hanoi in 1963 and not 1975, and what might have happened in Taiwan, and with what consequences, if we had walked away from Vietnam twelve years earlier?

One can wonder too how the Japanese might have reacted to an Asia effectively under Chinese hegemony in the mid '60s.

It is easy, of course, to postulate "what ifs" in support of a particular position that can never be disproved. But I simply do not believe that the situation in Asia today—the economic and political maturity of most of the non-communist countries, our satisfactory relations with China and its burgeoning capitalism, all of which by anyone's calculations must be considered to our advantage—would be nearly so favorable had we not stayed in South Vietnam.

In the late '60s, Senator Aiken made his famous, facetious suggestion that we simply declare we had won and leave. Not, in retrospect, too far from what actually happened. What is arguable is whether we did it soon enough. The irony is that when finally we did, and defeat was snatched from the jaws of victory by a confused, understandably antagonistic Congress, it really didn't matter much, not in the Far East anyway. When we made our commitment to South Vietnam in the late '50s and continued renewing it through the early '60s, there were real and valuable strategic reasons to do so. By the early '70s, these particular reasons had either ceased to exist or were markedly less important. Events nearby and further away as well had made the outcome of the game increasingly irrelevant.

Intellectual discussions aside, Vietnam was undeniably exciting. After five years on a campus, this was certainly my idea of the "real world," whatever that meant. Even without the war, it was a fascinating, utterly different experience—living in the complex, traditional countryside of a remote Asian country. With the war, there was an extra element of excitement, an adrenalin-producing high. It was different, of course, if you were a soldier in a combat unit. But for the rest of us, the war was there and yet strangely remote. The local

T. M. Deford

Vietnamese army captain takes you one morning into a village where two VC had been killed during the night, their bodies still there, awaiting his congratulations to the motley pack of village level soldiers and then you return to your compound where Australian cargo planes fly in supplies of beer, steaks, and other American necessities, twice a week. The next day, a Vietnamese tells you the two who had been killed were not VC at all, but personal enemies of the village chief, a contention the ARVN captain denies, his voice mixed with hurt at your mistrust and with anger too — for finding out the truth, or for unjustly accusing him?

A year or two later, I recall visiting a small village following a regional force sweep through an area in the province to the north—the one where the jets had come from; but except for the provincial capital and the airbase, most of that province, where President Thieu had been born, was still insecure. The soldiers had "captured" a middle-aged man, a VC cadre we were assured, and were questioning him in a reasonably brutal manner. He was sullen, surly, knew nothing, and in the end, they sort of lost interest. Presumably, he was what they said he was, but who knew and what difference did it make? They'd lock him up, they'd leave the village, and two days later, it would be "retaken" by his compatriots, another great victory. The irony, as always, was that the one great victory we did have, Tet 1968, was such a political and propaganda disaster that the military decimation of the VC was never accepted in the U.S. Crying wolf is a two-way street.

REFLECTIONS ON VIETNAM

Through it all, the Vietnamese went about their lives: they went to school, had girlfriends, married, and had children. One night, very shortly before the 1968 U.S. elections—when President Johnson was trying to persuade President Thieu to agree to negotiate and Thieu in turn was in contact with Nixon through an intermediary which made him disinclined to negotiate and Johnson knew it—a good Vietnamese friend of mine got married. His wife's family was quite rich: during any war, but especially this one, there are a lot of ways to make money. He was young, idealistic, anti-American—because of the effect our presence was increasingly having on the structure of his country—but strongly anti-communist. He was not handsome, nor particularly well-educated, but he had managed to find a truly beautiful, sophisticated, and rich wife. The wedding dinner would not have been out of place in New York, and when it was over, my champagne for the most part undrunk, I went back to the embassy to start reading the cables. It was morning now in Washington, and a very angry President Johnson was pulling out all the stops to force Thieu to accept the shape—for that's what it had come down to, *the shape*—of the negotiating table in Paris. It was not always easy to know who your friends were.

There was always pressure, if nothing else from the long hours of work. But there were rewarding moments even in the embassy. A three-nation group called the ICC remained in Saigon and Hanoi, overseeing, I believe, the forgotten Geneva accords of 1954, frozen in time as it were like some vestigial anatomical feature, whose purpose was now only divined by anthropologists. It consisted of Poland, Canada, and India, or perhaps Sweden. There was certainly no other official communist presence in Saigon in those days so it is hard to imagine how the Poles kept busy. Once a year, in any case, the Polish Ambassador to the ICC used to call on the American Ambassador (assuming he called on every other ambassador in Saigon once a year as well, he still had a lot of time on his hands).

In 1968, he chose as the day of annual call the day the Russians and the other Warsaw Pact countries invaded Czechoslovakia. In fact, presumably being the least-informed Polish diplomat in the world, he chose the exact hour the news was coming over the wires. I greeted him with a Reuters news dispatch which only referred to a Soviet invasion. Embarrassed, he said what was only too obvious, that he knew nothing. Twenty minutes later, when the next ticker came in, noting the Poles among the invasion force, I interrupted his meeting with the American Ambassador. Stammering apologies, wondering no doubt how in God's name he could find himself being informed by the U.S. Embassy in South Vietnam of his country's role in invading a communist ally, he departed. Better luck next year, Mr. Ambassador.

On Sundays in Saigon, we often drove to Vung Tau, an old French seaside resort several hours from Saigon, its beach-front villas mostly destroyed in earlier times. The road was safe if you got back before dark, and it was something of a diplomatic hangout on the weekend. One hotel was still open, literally a shell of its former self, but the sandy beach was wide and the water was very clean. Occasionally, there would be air strikes in the afternoon further up the coast as you lay on the beach, drinking Portuguese wine. Some of the third-world diplomats stayed overnight. The peppy middle-aged Brazilian Ambassador often did so with his two young Vietnamese girlfriends.

When I lived in the provinces, I could arrange a helicopter on weekends to go to Nha Trang, a large provincial capital of considerable beauty even then—wide quiet beaches, deserted islands, a tropical paradise in another time—but once or twice when I couldn't get away from my district, we'd go down in a few jeeps to the local beach: the district chief would post his soldiers around, and myself and a few adventurous Vietnamese would go swimming. But it was no Vung Tau.

Much later, I spent a week in a village deep in the delta, the flattest place I've ever seen: it was clearly in the dry season and the horizon stretched forever. The delta had its own beauty but it was too monotonous to be stimulating. The central part of South Vietnam where I had started was spectacularly beautiful with the mountains coming right down to the coast. Up until the 17th century, a good part of the coastal region had been controlled by a Hinduized civilization called Champa. There were still a considerable number of Cham temples along the coast, looking like smaller versions of Angkor Wat. One of the districts where I had worked was the last ethnic Cham area in the whole country. Champa had been a matriarchy. My assistant there, a seventeen-year

T. M. Deford

old kid, was a cousin of the woman who was the last, no doubt the very last, of the old royal family. I called on her once with my Cham assistant: she opened up an old wooden trunk and took out a small hammered gold crown and several heavy gold necklaces, put them on, and posed by an open window. The last of the line. Her nephew taught some of the local kids the Cham written language in a school paid for by U.S. aid. It was a complicated curlicue-type writing similar looking to Burmese; but his literacy in it was rudimentary. In the same village, shortly after I arrived, one of the soldiers had killed a tiger with an M-16. There had apparently been plenty of tigers there until the 1940s but this was the first anyone had seen in years and I never heard of another one.

The week I spent in the delta was an unusual one. I stayed there with several Vietnamese assistants but no other Americans. It was a thoroughly pacified area, in which the VC had never been able to make the slightest inroads, although surrounded by VC-controlled or infiltrated villages. My purpose in being there was to try to understand why. It was a magical week. The war didn't exist. The nearest airfield was some distance to the north and when the week ended, we left on a thin wooden motor boat through the back canals. We arrived late; the plane had come and gone and while I was waiting for it to return, I found a grubby little café nearby: five or six half-broken bar stools on a dirt floor, a few green and red plastic strips hanging down to form the door, and a cooler, the ice long since melted, filled with Cokes and Vietnamese beer. Two half-drunk popular force soldiers came up with a couple of dirty, blood-encrusted ears they wanted to sell me. The climax of a beautiful week.

Winter was the best season. It was dry and actually got cold enough for some Vietnamese to wear cotton sweaters in the early morning. On New Year's Eve, a tradition developed, the "Light at the End of the Tunnel" party. Because ours was a big house with a large garden, the party was held there. The first time was New Year's Eve 1967, or six weeks before the famous Tet attack. I remember coming downstairs New Year's Day about 8 o'clock on my way to the airport, and there were still several people from the night before lying around. One couple was dancing. The kind of party you have during a war.

A friend of mine, another one of the inhabitants of the house at that time, was back in Saigon this past year and knocked on the gate. The house is occupied now by a high-ranking South Vietnamese official who related how he infiltrated into our neighborhood several months before Tet as he was in charge of coordinating the Tet "uprising" after the attack had succeeded in Saigon. He had been holing up in some store several blocks away and may have heard the all-night festivities later. He invited my friend in: two former enemies, brought together by this house, whose original owner had been a mistress of Bao Dai, the last emperor of Vietnam. It was Tet 1988. The former Viet Cong leader served tea in the garden, and special holiday sweets, and then talked politely in French of the Vietnam War.

MISCARRIAGE: REFLECTIONS ON A WAR

🕉   William M. Drennen, Jr.

Flying low and fast over the terrain between 88 and 64 the slow rolling hills are dotted with tree stumps and winding dirt roads, big cities off to the left and sparkling lakes and one significant elevation—Vietnam. For whom of us in the Class of '64 was Vietnam not a landmark —we, who would change the world to make it a peaceful, verdant paradise, found life head-on at war, stark contrast to idealized visions of freedom and optimism of Yale's academic enclaves.

For some of us the war was journalism, for some of us it was protest, for most of us it was avoidance. For none of us it was nothing. Our personalities all are marked with scars of our interaction with history in the Indochinese peninsula.

In 1964 as "Classified Material Officer" on a WWII vintage LST, I was filing a secret memo that warned all commanders to "... be on alert for anti-Vietnam rallies on October 10 in ports around the world." That message struck me as singularly curious—anti-Vietnam rallies? What could that mean?

Not long after that we were confronted with "The

Maddox" incident and Johnson's escalation of the war. There were calls for volunteers for "Swift Boats." I liked the name. I was bored wallowing around on that old LST. "The Dodge County" (LST 722) would have been my one and only duty station had I followed my original intention to serve out a two-year NROTC obligation. Carroll Cavanagh and several other classmates were stationed with the amphibious Navy in Little Creek, Virginia. It was a good life—sex, booze, and cruise —but it was not real enough. It was boring.

So I signed up to go to Vietnam—find out what it was all about. That was August of 1965. In December, my orders were in. Go to San Diego for six months counterinsurgency training. What a deal. A bachelor pad in Coronado, temporary duty without watches, guerrilla warfare training in the desert, "SERE" (Survival, Evasion, Resistance, and Escape). I learned how to eat rattlesnake and fly; how to kill a white rabbit with one blow; how to survive being stuffed in a shoebox for two hours; and how to speak enough Vietnamese to flag down a sampan in the delta.

One useful thing I did learn in language school is that fifteen well-disciplined Marine recruits can learn a lot more Vietnamese than a portly, alcoholic, Ivy-League graduate who is more interested in learning how to fly an airplane than to converse in Vietnamese.

Halfway through my training in San Diego I was struck by the fact that I was not on a track to take command of a Swift Boat. I was being trained for MACV (Military Assistance

Command, Vietnam). MACV meant I would be assigned as an advisor to a Vietnamese unit such as the "Junk Boats" (wooden motor-sailers for coastal interdiction), "Riverines" (theoretically armored landing and support craft for amphibious landings in the delta), or most likely, paperwork in Saigon.

I went to the personnel officer and told him that was not what I had volunteered for or been promised by the Bureau of Naval Personnel in Washington. I wanted to command, not advise. If I couldn't get a Swift Boat or something similar, then by God I was not extending and they could turn me loose right now.

They found a way. I was assigned to PBRs.

What's a PBR?

Patrol Boat River—a small, light, fast, shallow-draft vessel capable of disrupting Viet Cong "communications" in the Mekong Delta by denying them the use of the waterways. A PBR had a 31-foot fiberglass hull with twin six-cylinder diesel engines powering twin "Jacuzzi" pumps, the same pump found in your hot tub. The pumps worked like water-jet propulsion, taking in water from beneath the boat and pushing it out the back.

These little boats were armed with twin fifty-caliber machine guns in a turret in the front, a fifty-caliber machine gun and a Honeywell grenade launcher aft, an M-60 machine gun mounted on one of the armor plates amidships, plus M-16s and grenade launchers for anybody else who had a trigger finger working. The boats would patrol in pairs in the canals and rivers of the delta and keep "charlie" from doing his dirty work. They were also great for water-skiing and tiger hunting. If you saw *Apocalypse Now* you saw PBRs.

My new assignment meant I would have to go to San Francisco for six more weeks of training. What a shame. San Francisco in the summer of 1966: smoke-ins on the courthouse steps, concerts in Golden Gate Park, free love by way of North Beach and the hip generation. What does a liberal-leaning, Yale-educated Navy Lieutenant feel about Vietnam in this environment?

Nothing. Counterinsurgency training was like summer camp with history lessons, economic theory, and popular psychology thrown in with cookouts, capture the flag, and target practice with real guns. It was practical and interesting and might be useful if the United States ever got itself invaded or West Virginia decided to secede from the Union. Vietnam had very little to do with me.

For one thing I knew we were in trouble in Vietnam when the first day of class the instructor, a "vet" from the war zone, told us that communism was bad because people don't have any freedom, that the U.S. and South Vietnam refused to abide by the 1954 Geneva Accords to hold free elections in 1963 because the Viet Cong would win, and that Asians don't care as much about life as Americans do.

What has that got to do with Freedom?

Basically I knew the war was wrong, but I was curious. Throughout the summer of 1966 I rode my motorcycle

William M. Drennen, Jr.

around Berkeley, smoked dope, drank wine, went to light shows and rock concerts at the Fillmore, and hung out in the "Haight" on weekends. During the week I played war games in the marshes in the north end of San Francisco Bay.

Then suddenly one day I was at Travis Air Force Base—July 30, 1966. Amid the departing chaos of young boys from moms and dads and young men from howling babies and stifling wives, and brave sad smiles, I said good-bye to Merrill Pasco, who had watched my schizophrenic summer and driven me to Travis to see me off. The drama of the moment, of saying good-bye to friends, to your country, to go somewhere to fight a war, is a cliché. A rich, powerful cascade of relentless emotion, a send-off, and not unlike a funeral. And then there is that loneliness that follows, chasing the falling sun across the wide Pacific, so high, and wondering why.

After a stopover in Honolulu, we arrived at Clark Air Base in the Philippines just past time to catch the last training mission for a week. My clock started for "rotation" purposes on July 30, so I would be eligible to go back to the States anytime after July 1, 1967. From the attitude of the training command at the little jungle warfare school at Subic Bay, you would have thought I had stolen Fort Knox, spending an extra week in the Philippines with nothing to do but sightsee, eat, drink, and get laid, all at government expense.

The jungle training was taught by "Negritos," tiny little native Filipinos wise in the ways of the jungle. After they showed us how to jab for crawdads with pointy little sticks and make leaky shelters out of bamboo, they spent the rainy nights under plastic and fished with goggles on. After three days of constant rain with no poncho, I was glad when they put us on a C130 for Saigon.

The opening scene from *Platoon* was exactly the way I remember Tan Son Nhut Air Base the day I arrived. I didn't see any body bags, just long aluminum canisters. There was a lot of stuff going on, and wind and dust and confusion and waiting, and these funny looking airplanes called "Caribou" which seemed to take off without any runway. I saw a lot of Caribou in Vietnam, and I never did see much runway. Runways had the unfortunate characteristics of being large, stationary targets that required their users to follow strict glide paths. The Caribou could jump almost up and down on a postage stamp, but the VC loved to lob mortars on that postage stamp.

I never did find out why they were called Caribou. Certainly not for that useful, slow-moving asset of the Vietnamese farmer, the ubiquitous water buffalo. Water buffalo didn't do much jumping up and down—just slow, patient plodding before the cone-headed plowman in the picturesque sunsets of the delta.

I spent the first month and a half of my tour at Cat Lo, the Navy's staging point for the PBR river patrols for the ship channel to Saigon. The harbor at Vung Tau was also the off-loading point for the boats being shipped in from the States. As each squadron of men was assembled, trained, and delivered to Vietnam, ten boats were supposed to meet them there. Five of River Patrol Squadron 523's boats arrived when we did. The other five did not come in until six weeks later. I was assigned to wait for them.

After recovering from a bout of dengue fever, a mild form of malaria, and watching half of my squadron head off up the Mekong towards Long Xuyen, I started volunteering for patrols. My first patrol was an all-nighter on the ship channel. We left the base at Cat Lo at dusk, firing our machine guns into the "Free fire Zone" of the marsh on the way out across the bay. We headed up the channel eating C rations and watching the sunset over the mangrove swamps.

I'm not afraid to tell you I was scared. I *was* scared. I was not afraid of dying. I was afraid of getting captured or messing my drawers or doing something uncool. All night long we drifted in the current of that narrow channel, avoiding ships carrying goods to Saigon, listening to the thunder of B-52s dropping devastation on the distant mountains, watching the red spray from Puff the Magic Dragon's mini-guns watering down a VC stronghold. Every night was fireworks somewhere in the delta, and the delta was flat enough that one could enjoy the show from just about any location.

As the night paled into dawn, the dark silhouettes of the banks gave way to a stark moonscape of marsh and swampland defoliated by MACV's Agent Orange spray program. The lush mangrove had become a bleak mud flat with bits of gray wood poking up here and there. And out in it, breaking off scraps of firewood for the evening cook fire, a handful of peasants with gray beards and skinny legs and cone-shaped hats trying to ignore the war going on around them. While we were on patrol DC3s flew over, laying down another line of defoliant.

I also made patrols with some Swift Boat guys. They would do 24-hour patrols of 20-30 mile areas of the delta coastline. The patrols were long, the water choppy, and life at best unpleasant. I also went out with the Coast Guard, which had stationed cutters, somewhat larger than the Swift Boats, in Vietnam. They patrolled a little further from the beach and were another line of defense against Viet Cong resupply from the sea. Their patrols were three days long with even less happening, but superior meals. The coastal blockade was so effective the North Vietnamese built the Ho Chi Minh Trail to supply the troops in the south. The Navy had done such a good job that coastal patrols were boring. I was glad to be on the river.

Once our squadron was assembled and established at Long Xuyen, I began making patrols on the upper reaches of the Bassac River. Our patrol area was a three-hour ride up river from the base. During the fall of 1966, the monsoon rains had so flooded the delta that behind the tree-lined banks of the river, the Mekong Delta was one huge lake. The grass huts gathered in hamlets along the river banks had water flowing through the windows, and families of six or eight were perched in hammocks above flood level. As our mean green machines lumbered up the rivers, the wakes from the water-jet engines wet bottoms, knocked over pig pens, and did little to win friends.

I taught English for a while in a school in Long Xuyen. The students of all ages were eager and excited learners. I didn't know or care about their politics. I cared about them. Teaching and making medical calls on villages and hamlets was the most meaningful and important work I did in a year. But I am sure I lost more potential friends in the wake of our patrol boat than I would have made in a whole year of school teaching or medical visits.

The number one lesson in counterinsurgency training is the importance of winning the hearts and minds of the people. As soon as American units began arriving in Vietnam, those lessons flew away. If each U.S. soldier had made ten Vietnamese friends while he was there, we could have won the hearts and the minds—and the war; but we were too insecure and uptight to make friends. We just wanted to beat up on them.

One morning, our patrol of two boats was ordered to go through a narrow canal between the Bassac and the Mekong. There was no way to turn the boat around if there was trouble. The villagers were just getting up, bathing in the canal, close enough to shake hands on either side. Bright sun rising through the morning mist, rice paddies for miles on either side. Death felt very close on that bright morning. Living was real.

There was a hospital in Long Xuyen manned by an Australian medical team, including nurses. Between patrols we hung out with the Aussies, danced at the Army Officers Club, drank and played volleyball. Quite civilized really, and somewhat surreal. We had *cyclo* races around town, took pleasure cruises in our PBRs, played cribbage and chess, made up songs. At one point my roommate, a Princetonian from St. Louis named Harry Weber, began putting together the score for a musical we were going to call "The OK Canal." Once the VC started shooting at us, we got more serious and the musical was never produced.

River Patrol Squadron 523 consisted of ten boats, each with a four-man crew, seven patrol officers, operations center staff, and some engineers to keep things running. We ran four, fifteen-hour, two-boat patrols a day. I went out as a patrol officer three to four times a week, and did four- or eight-hour watches in the operations center when I wasn't on patrol.

Patrol consisted of running up river to Chau Doc, reading intelligence reports for suspected VC activity at the Special Forces base there, then motoring up to the Cambodian border and drifting downstream all night, or searching sampans all day. Anybody on the river was subject to search, and if they tried to avoid the search, we were supposed to shoot them.

In the delta the rivers and canals were the roads. Try to imagine for a minute what your own life would be like if anytime you wanted to go to the store, or to visit a friend, or to see a movie, some foreigner in an armored police car was liable to pull you over, ask you where you were going, check your ID, and search your car. That is what we did. That was our job.

Eventually, Vietnamese policemen were put on the boats to do the questioning and searching. That felt a little more courteous, although I was never sure that the police weren't VC controlled. In ten months of patrols three times a week, I never once found any Viet Cong suspects or supplies or materiel. That doesn't mean that our boats didn't get shot at or turn up Viet Cong, or arrest some suspicious people. I just wasn't there when it happened.

Several times a week we would get shot at from the beach. During one stretch in early 1967, our boats were involved in twenty-four fire fights in eighteen days. If we were getting that much attention I figured we must have been doing something to irritate the VC. We, as river warriors, weren't heavily into body counts and that sort of thing. If we got shot at or someone tried to avoid a search we would chase them as best we could, shoot up the village, or sink their sampans. But we (I) didn't go ashore. If we were attacked, we shot back, cleared the area and called for helicopter gunships or artillery. That is why I loved the Navy. We had good clean routes of escape. We had our own air force. And the VC had no way to chase us.

My baptism by fire came during that period, in broad daylight. We were heading up a channel behind an island in the Ham Luong River when the sound of sticks cracking and the sight of stones skipping announced an ambush. "Walking machine gun to starboard!" Then everything was drowned out by the sound of six fifty-caliber machine guns raking the tree line, me screaming into the radio for helicopter support, and the twin diesels churning up the shallow water. *Di di mau!* (Go, go fast!)

I felt exhilarated after we had cleared the area. No one was hurt. I had been shot at, I had shot back, and I had not shit. Two weeks later another patrol was ambushed at the same location with a 57mm recoilless rifle, sinking one boat, killing five people and wounding six. They were my friends, but I felt totally detached. Just one of those stupid things that happen.

During one R & R visit to Saigon in early 1967, a friend of mine from San Diego introduced me to two Vietnamese girls who were working in the BOQ. They were pleasant and funny and talkative and "cultured." They lived with their mother and another brother and sister in a little apartment on the fourth floor of a building near the Vietnamese palace, walking distance from the BOQ. My friend had been dating Kim, the pretty older sister (24), who had kept herself beautiful in the traditional Vietnamese way: thin face and body and long flowing black hair. She always wore an *ao dai*, the elegant flowered pants-skirt native to Vietnam.

Dung (Zum), the younger sister, was obviously more intelligent in a Western way. She wore miniskirts, traded jokes with the bachelors in the BOQ, spoke and understood most English idiom, and was a delightful companion. We played Chinese checkers and dominoes at the family apartment, we danced to the Mommas and the Poppas, we drank rice wine, and we laughed—laughed at our attempts to bridge the communication gap.

My Vietnamese was atrocious. Dung was a good teacher and friend during my infrequent visits to Saigon. Then she came to visit me in Long Xuyen where her uncle was Province Chief, and our relationship changed. In April I got a letter from her saying she was pregnant, that she loved me, that she wanted to have a son for me. To please take care of her and our baby.

In June my orders came to return to the States and be separated from the Navy. My time was up. No re-enlistment. No Antarctica. No more Navy. Just good-bye. Say good-night, Gracie.

I made my way to Saigon and checked back into the Hotel Victoria where I had stayed my first night in country and had first seen the war from the rooftop.

I called Dung.

We had dinner together at the Arc En Ciel, Cholon's most famous restaurant. Afterwards, we went back to my room at the Victoria. Dung was obviously pregnant. I gave her a diamond ring I had bought at the PX that afternoon for $110. I had no idea what to do or say, so I drank Pernod and smoked some dope I had bought in Hong Kong the month before. Dung just looked at me with those sad black eyes while I sank into unconsciousness. Sometime during the night she left.

I have often imagined dialogues I might have had that night, but didn't. I was glad she was carrying my baby, leaving my mark in a far-off corner of the world. I wasn't willing to take any responsibility for it. It was just one of those things that happened. She would have to learn to take care of herself.

Dung's black eyes spoke for her. "Why don't you take me with you. Why can't we talk about some real future, not this shabby thing about this diamond ring being you through eternity and always there. Don't you understand? I am carrying your baby. Your child. Your child is going to be born in this country, and you are leaving me no offers, no hope, just good-bye. You run off and be crazy man, but I am real, I am a real person here, a girl five months ago with hope and a smile and an aptitude for language who was attracted to you, and let you have your way with me. Now I am pregnant with an American baby. Who will look after me? Who will look after our child when you are gone? You are crazy man. You are something inhuman I don't understand."

"Maybe someday when I get settled down I will send for you and the baby. Right now I am just confused and unhappy and feeling guilty and I need to clear my mind. I need some space to think about things. I need to catch up with the world that's spinning round out there with Beatles and Stones. I need to go to rock concerts and anti-war rallies. I need to know where I fit, if my 'outlaw' theory is honest. When America is so screwed up that it would destroy a country in order to make it safe for democracy, I will not recognize laws or submit to being governed by such a social system. Let the LSD generation rule the world. I want to be free.

"But maybe when the war is over I will come back and you can be my mistress. And everything will be all right. Call me if you need me. Good-bye."

The next morning I got a cab to Tan Son Nhut Air Base. Twelve hours later I was on a plane to Japan.

On August 7, 1967, I resigned from active duty at Treasure Island Naval Station in San Francisco Bay. I had already begun a full-fledged dive into the elusive nirvana of drugs. I had left my soul in San Francisco when I went to Vietnam, and when I got back I couldn't find it. These chemicals— these fast, easy cures for unenlightenment—nurtured my search. I smoked marijuana and hashish, took uppers and downers and psychedelics. I traveled Europe and the Middle East and Canada searching for a soul, a way of life that made sense. The further I went, the more drugs I took, the less sense anything made.

Finally, three months in a French prison sobered me up, gave me time to read and reflect, and got my life started again. At some point during my crazed odyssey I received this letter at the American Express office in Rome:

> *Dear Bill,*
> *I am sorry to tell you that I went horseback riding at my Uncle's in Da Lat and have miscarriage. Write me.*
> *Dung*

A LETTER ON VIETNAM

%   John S. Wilbur, Jr.

Dear Greeley:
After much delay, I am sending you my written thoughts on Vietnam as you requested. I hope that in combination with others whom you solicited they will form a rough mosaic of what and how Vietnam was to the Class of '64. In doing so, how could I forget that it was from your [Bob Kaiser's] home in Washington, D.C., that I left on my second abbreviated tour. In fact John Hollister-Stein drove me that beautiful spring day; and it was again to your home that I returned one very early morning in late August of 1968.

Some two days before, now over twenty years ago, I had lifted off from Tan Son Nhut in a packed 707, a bright orange Braniff disco-job. As soon as we had cleared Vung Tao and were unalterably into the South China Sea, the captain came on the speaker and told us he wanted us to know how proud he and America were of us, how tough they had known it was, and in particular, thanks for a job well done.

With that he pulled a hard bank to the east and off we soared "to the world." It was the only, and as nice a speech as I was ever to hear about Vietnam. Everyone cheered. Happy faces looked at each other in a moment of disbelief.

It was over. There were going to be no more "blow out experiences," no more everyday weird chaos of emotions: fear, pride, disgust, hatred, terror, sadness, and wonder all before sunset each day. No more stomach-gripping shock of destruction, emptiness of killing, wonder of sorrow, disbelief, and confusion and on and on. No more Vietnam.

No sooner did this reality descend, than the onset of something even more obscure and more ominous emerged. If not Vietnam—then what? What now? I will never forget staring off into the clouds as we crossed the Pacific with no idea, whatsoever, of what was going to become of me.

Anyone sent back and dumped at Clark Air Base with an empty bus waiting realized or began to realize that troubling sensation. There was nowhere to avoid it. From tough or at least brazen survivors of early manhood, we suddenly became veterans. Veterans of the lost war, old shoes the nation having worn was ready to discard. Our ceremony was the signing of chits for the return of gear. DEROSSED by mail, people looked at us with a mixture of embarrassment and consternation as we awkwardly stared at the loose, unraveled ends of our young indefinite lives.

Like Rip Van Winkle, here we are in 1988 awakened after a twenty-year slumber. Dan Quayle became the slap on the face to stir us. Those who never confronted the national attention of wondering where *they* were during "the conflict"

John S. Wilbur, Jr.

for a moment, at least, are looking furtively at each other and to the left and right. Almost on top of that came your call asking some of us who were there to write our thoughts for the 25th. As we talked, I believe there was a wry comment that there weren't very many of us to choose from and certainly few authors amidst those.

Because Yale was to provide the context, it particularly reminds me of a memory or rather a flood of them on one particular night, still as bright in my head as the moon above the rough tidal edge of the South China Sea, the "Free-Fire Secret Zone" coast of Kien Hoa, IV Corps, Mekong Delta, summer of 1967, pre-Tet.

It was one of many nights when wrapped up inside a cocoon of self, trying to vent the chaos of struggling feelings I would compose my letter to Kingman Brewster. Poor Kingman, he would never know what a target he had become in my mind. It was born from the head-shaking absurdity of lying wet-bellied in the mud, drenched with sweat and bug repellent, hooded in mosquito netting, swollen hands nervously rubbing the slick armalite AR-16, staring across a tidal stream into the bottomless dark of the mangroves waiting to kill with premeditation whatever human being we all fervently hoped would inexorably wander into our diligently contrived death trap.

Dear Kingman:

Needed: more Yalemen. Where are they? I know they have their reasons, most of them very under-

standable and many very acceptable except that we need them badly just now.

It's not that this can't be done by others, it's just that it's so screwed up over here that we need the ones that you can count on and trust that they won't screw up and do the wrong thing. Over here, there is no doing the right thing. No one from Westmoreland down does that. What's really essential is not doing the wrong thing.

It seems to me that the only option in navigating the terrible choices of war is to search deeply into what one was taught, told, or shown and stay desperately close to that. To be a Yaleman may be a vague notion of fictional intangibles without much to describe, but here in war it's simple and inescapably clear. It means: not bungling into killing, guarding against the cruelty in carelessness, understanding the fear in the hand on the gun, caring always for one's victims, steeling oneself to stop unnecessary destruction, finding the guts to back it up, never letting cynicism get the upper hand, and finally, never stop trying to avoid the "wrong thing."

Those are the lessons that I know I have learned from among many sources maybe, but certainly and unmistakably from Yale. I know I picked them up somewhere from the buildings, fields, classes, books, teachers, students, and friends. So where are the other

John S. Wilbur, Jr.

guys, Kingman? Where are those guys? We need them right away, if not on the flank, at least behind, ready to back us up. If you don't get them over here, then take your award when the responsibility for this mess is passed out. You want to bitch about burned hooches, screaming kids, wailing women, and little dead men light as rag dolls? They're yours too.

Yours truly, John S. Wilbur, Jr., *Lt.JG, USN (R), Vietnam.*

That night we "egressed" out without killing anyone or anything: disappointed. Even if we thought we weren't, at least God was ahead.

Those indelible thoughts sank deeply into me like a litany. For all the sophomore emotion in which they were couched, I'm surprised after all these years that what I just wrote is almost an exact memory.

If it weren't for Mac Deford and Eddie Trippe and a few others out there, I could have slipped a little bit too deeply into that monsoon world. What it did for me, or to me, is what I've got somewhere still rattling around. Every now and then it comes out in a statement, thought, glance, action, or attitude. I've never quite put my finger on it, sort of lost interest. It seems to come out in a kind of blur in direction, or objective, a recurrent indecision to follow or commit to the better traveled way, a sporadic inclination to exhibit an uninspired "give a shit" turn of the eye, or "fuck it" hunch of the shoulder indifference.

REFLECTIONS ON VIETNAM

But now we have our own Cabinet seat for Veterans Affairs, too many books and movies, even a prime-time TV series. Somebody is out there trying to glorify us with awards and attention. Heroes are only some on whom other people pin medals. I'm proud to say I know a few with and without. The rest of us are too far gone to care what people did or didn't do, or even what we did or didn't do. It's really quite long ago. Other wars were far more impressive, important, and history-worthy.

All I really know is every now and then driving through south Florida, on a late afternoon, with the sprawling land spreading flat as an anvil to the west, with clouds for mountains, I sometimes see in its place, rice paddies, delta-brown canals, and thatched-roofed hamlets. Then I remember the warmth and grace of the people, the rhythmic cycle of harvest and planting, the busy passage of river life; and I'd kind of like to go back and never have to do again what I thought I had to do before.

Mingo

BRUCE

🙵 Mimo Robinson

I was only twenty-two when I stood by the side of the road in that small town in Maine watching the parade go by, a parade commemorating all the young men who had died fighting for Uncle Sam. I was a widow. I had been married when I was twenty. He was my childhood sweetheart, a blond, blue-eyed, broad-shouldered young man with his high ideals and grand expectations of teaching and coaching in his old school once he had "come to the aid of his country." We had needed to be together and had married as soon as he had graduated from college.

I watched the crusty old man, Ralph Cline, walk by, erect and tall, leading the parade in his World War I uniform, which, 40 years later, still fit him just fine. Is that how Bruce would have felt in the year 2000, proudly sporting his jungle fatigues at the head of a parade? Would he then have had the unwavering belief in the necessity of that war as this old guy obviously had in his? After having lived through the heat, the filth, the deception, and the disillusion of a year in South Vietnam fighting a war for which no one seemed remotely grateful, it's difficult to imagine him feeling anything but hurt. But then, that is my disillusion, not his. I wasn't there . . . maybe there had been times of laughing and camaraderie and moments of heroism like on *M*A*S*H* that would overshadow the rest in future years. But I remember the letter that I got when he had only been there for two months telling me about the death of a good friend who had been at Quantico with us, and I think of his pain. Despite these losses, though, Bruce never questioned his country's actions.

Next in line after Ralph was the 4H Club, shiny young men and women with a firm understanding of the land, the birth of a calf, and how to produce alfalfa in Maine soil to feed their sheep. They looked so innocent.

My mind wandered back to the hospital at Clark Air Base in the Philippines where I, as next of kin, had been sent by the Marine Corps to be with my beautiful young husband after he had been seriously wounded by a number of sniper's bullets during a late-night volunteer mission. That body that had, during college, been so firm, so agile, that he'd been made captain of the baseball team, that body that had come to its maximum capacity for fitness during basic training at Quantico, Virginia, was now prone in a rotating hospital bed, pierced and torn, sewn together again, half strung up and half held down . . . and for what?

Ah, here comes the school band now in their green and white uniforms playing the tuba and the trombone. Do they know what they're playing? Do they know what "Anchors

Away" really means? And there's Mrs. Haskell, the story lady from the library. She must be seventy now . . . and there's the little Carey girl as Little Red Riding Hood. . . . They're all there. Those wonderful stories where good triumphs over evil. When does that really happen?

I easily found myself back on the troop transport plane going toward Clark. I was scared and alone and the only one aboard this plane who was not a young soldier on his way into the rice paddies. Of course this plane was without benefit of movies, airplane snacks, or a portable bar; it gave all the more time for gazing at a photograph of a girlfriend or fingering a rosary. They hesitantly asked me what I was doing there, although I'm sure, most already knew.

The parade had turned down the hill toward the water. This part had made me cry every Memorial Day, even when I knew nothing of war except what I had read in *For Whom the Bell Tolls*. I watched as Hugo Lettinen flew over in his sea plane and dropped a wreath on the water. Hugo was the one who was known to have had an intimate relationship with a woman on one of the islands here. He would fly out to see her in his plane. He apparently arrived one day unannounced and found her in bed with another man. He was said to have quietly gathered up all their clothes, left the house, gone back into the air and from the window of the plane strewn the clothes out over the harbor. Possibly it was with that same sense of revenge that he now threw the wreath from that same window. When it was floating on the water the uniformed men in the parade raised their rifles to their shoulders and fired three times.

The crack of the gunfire brought me back to Clark. Bruce's brother Aldy met me there. I don't think I could have made it through without him. We shared the hurt of watching one we loved in so much pain. We shared the knowledge that there was nothing we could do to help. We also shared the estrangement we felt from this person who had seen a whole section of life and death that we had never seen. We could walk the halls of the hospital together when Bruce was asleep and talk to the burn cases or help them write letters home. We could look in at the spinal cord injuries together, those who would never function by themselves again and feel lucky that Bruce's injuries were so "light." I felt so inadequate with my bedside gaiety or sadness; I felt so young and inexperienced in dealing with emotions such as these; I felt so robbed of the carefree joy of early marriage. Thank God Aldy was there to smooth over my mistakes. I had been away from this young husband of mine more than I had been with him. He had been gone for 11 months. Our letters had been plentiful, but the lines of true communication couldn't withstand the reality of our very different worlds. He had written about Hue and Da Nang and about his R & R in Hong Kong. He had written about friends and commanding officers and tanks and fears. I had written about work and friends and family and gatherings. We had needed to see each other to bridge the separation. But the long awaited reunion was clouded over by pain and sadness.

The parade was making its way back up the hill, away from the sea, toward the AmVets Hall where the final speeches would be given. At the end of the parade were the town's two recently polished fire engines from which a few volunteers in duty garb were throwing candy to the onlooking kids.

As I walked back up the hill I remembered walking outside St. Alban's Hospital on Long Island. Bruce had been discharged from Clark; he seemed to be progressing well and they were scared of infection. We all knew they also needed his bed. The family was elated with the news. Finally he would come home.

"Cardiac arrest in 302. Cardiac arrest in 302." Bruce died on March 13, 1966; his second kidney had failed. As Scott Davis, the young boy from down the street, played taps on his bugle, I allowed myself to cry once more.

There have been other times through the years that I have cried about Bruce, but now, twenty years later, even more than crying, I would like to talk to him. Assuming that he, too, would have twenty years of perspective, I would like to know his thoughts and his feelings. I would like him to know my husband and my children. I would like to be able to sit down with him and, together, find peace.

December 9, 1985

A NOTE ON CONTRIBUTORS

T. M. (Mac) Deford

Mac Deford was a Foreign Service Officer when he was in Vietnam from 1966 to 1969. He subsequently studied Arabic in Beirut and was posted in Saudi Arabia and Jordan. He resigned from the State Department in 1977 to join Merrill Lynch, where he currently is the head of private banking in Asia. He lives in Hong Kong with his wife, Zehra; their son, Benjie, is at boarding school in the States.

William M. Drennen, Jr.

Two years after leaving the Navy, Bill Drennen handed his guilt back to Satan, his bedroll to the Goddess of Love at Woodstock, and dropped back into life as a mild-mannered filmmaker first in Washington, D.C., then in West Virginia, where he now serves in perfect freedom as the Commissioner of Culture and History.

Robert G. Kaiser

Bob Kaiser is Managing Editor of The Washington Post and author, most recently, of *Why Gorbachev Happened, His Triumphs and His Failure.*

Mimo Robinson

Mimo Robinson is a painter. She lives in the White Mountains of New Hampshire with her husband Sam, and their three almost-grown children.

John S. Wilbur, Jr.

John Wilbur is a Florida trial lawyer and counselor: "In my youth, I pursued the life of experience. It took me to foreign lands and Vietnam. I am thankful for the latter for developing a better man of me, with sadness as well as wisdom. As a mature man I married and am grateful for the growth of its magnificent emotions and insights. Now if I can maintain the continuing benefits of what has been forged in me thus far, I look forward to the best and last."

COLOPHON

About the Type

Headlines and text type were set in Adobe Garamond, adapted by Robert Slimbach from Claude Garamond's original 16th-century designs for the roman lettering and from the designs of Robert Granjon, Garamond's younger colleague, for the italic. The title on the cover and on the title page and initial capitals were set in Caslon Open Face, based on the designs of the 18th-century English designer William Caslon. Tracery on the cover is from a 16th-century bookplate engraving by Oronce Finé. The title page logo was drawn by Raúl Soltan.

About the Book

Kate Siepmann/EDIGRAPH, of West Lebanon, New Hampshire, designed this keepsake volume, the first book produced and published by Dialogue Press. It was composed entirely on the desktop. Jethro K. Lieberman was compositor and editor; Tracy A. Smith was editorial assistant. Text was typed in WordPerfect 5.1 and imported into PageMaker 4.0 running under Windows. Pages were proofed on an HP Laser III and output in Postscript on RC1200 by Digital Pre-Press in New York City. Cover stock is Curtis Tweedweave Duplex; the text paper is 80# Mohawk Cream White Satin. It was printed and bound in a limited edition of 1,500 copies by Northlight Studio Press in Barre, Vermont.

About Dialogue Press

Principals of Dialogue Press are Tom Goldstein, Michael L. Keiser, and Jethro K. Lieberman.